BEARS

CONTENTS

Bears huge and hairy	4–5
Loving mothers	6–7
Sweet-toothed bears	8–9
Winter sleep	10–11
Bears great and small	12–13
A humpbacked fisherman	14–15
Going where they please	16–17
A bear with a mask	18–19
Life on the ice	20–21
A mane with a collar	22–23
A termite eater	24–25
The smallest of all	26–27
Of bears and men	28–29
Glossary	30
Index	31

DB DM

Original title of the book in Spanish:
El Fascinante Mundo de... Los Osos.
© Copyright Parramón Ediciones, S.A.
Published by Parramón Ediciones, S.A., Barcelona, Spain.

Author: Maria Ángels Julivert
Illustrations: Marcel Socías Studios

English text © Copyright 1995 by Barron's Educational
Series, Inc.

All inquiries should be addressed to:
Barron's Educational Series, Inc.
250 Wireless Boulevard
Hauppauge, NY 11788-3917

ISBN: 0-8120-9422-0

Library of Congress Catalog Card No. 95-3154

Library of Congress Cataloging-in-Publication Data

Julivert, Maria Ángels.
  [Fascinante mundo de los osos. English]
  The fascinating world of—bears / by Maria Ángels Julivert ;
illustrations by Marcel Socías Studios.—1st ed.
    p. cm.
  Includes index.
  ISBN 0-8120-9422-0
  1. Bears—Juvenile literature. [1. Bears.] I. Marcel Socías
  Studios. II. Title.
QL737.C27J8513 1995
599.74'446—dc20   95-3154
                                                   CIP
                                                   AC

Printed in Spain
5678 9960 987654321

THE FASCINATING WORLD OF...

BEARS

by

Maria Ángels Julivert

Illustrations by Marcel Socías Studios

FOREST HOUSE ®

School & Library Edition

BEARS HUGE AND HAIRY

These big mammals have **corpulent** bodies and enormous heads. Their eyes, in contrast, are small; they have round ears and a very short tail.

The bear's heavy body is covered with thick **fur**, with color varying from one **species** to another. Some bears have light patches on certain parts of the body.

Their paws are very short, and have five toes armed with sharp, pointed claws. These are powerful weapons that they use to defend themselves and to attack their prey. They also use them to dig up vegetation, to climb trees, or to tear off bark.

Like humans, bears are **plantigrades**, which means that they walk by pressing their heels against the ground. They move about on all fours, but they are capable of standing up on their hind legs and maintaining their balance. They can even cover short distances like this.

They like water a lot and they are excellent swimmers. Some also climb trees. Despite their weight and their apparently clumsy gait, bears are quite agile, and when necessary, can run fast.

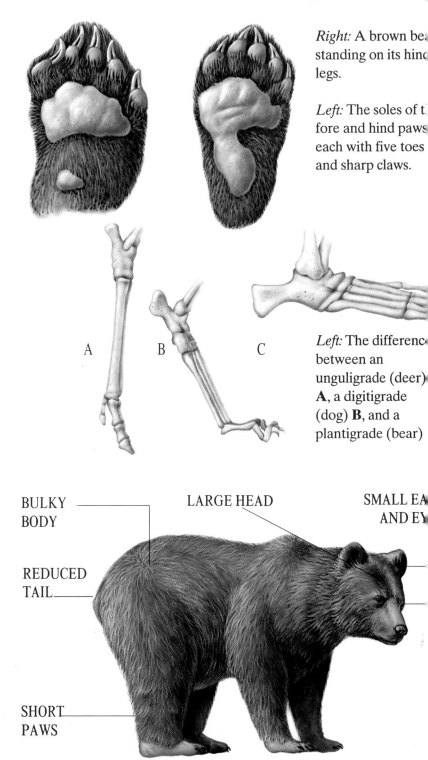

Right: A brown bear standing on its hind legs.

Left: The soles of the fore and hind paws each with five toes and sharp claws.

A   B   C

Left: The difference between an unguligrade (deer) **A**, a digitigrade (dog) **B**, and a plantigrade (bear)

BULKY BODY

LARGE HEAD

SMALL EARS AND EYES

REDUCED TAIL

SHORT PAWS

LOVING MOTHERS

Bears are solitary animals, but at certain times of the year, usually in spring, they congregate to form pairs.

During this period, there can be confrontations between males fighting for a female. Rivals exchange menacing signals to intimidate their opponents: they bare their teeth and emit low growls. If this does not have the desired effect, the bears start a savage fight until one of them gives up and runs away.

The pair will stay together, **mating** for a very short time, only a few days. During the period of winter **hibernation**, between one and four young will be born, with their eyes shut and without **fur** (except polar bear cubs). The cubs are very small and defenseless, and weigh between 7.1 and 21.2 ounces (200–600 g). As soon as they are born, the mother licks their bodies clean.

In spring, the mother and her young will leave their **den**. The cubs are still small and they follow their mothers everywhere. The female looks after them alone, protects them, and shows them how to look for food and how to protect themselves. When they are two or three years old, the young bears are at last able to fend for themselves and they begin their independent lives.

In regions where the climate is warmer, the young can be born at any time of the year.

Above: The cubs already know how climb trees, and sometimes, when they are frightene they hide among t branches of a tree.

Left: The cubs are born defenseless t they grow quickly, nourished by their mother's milk.

Right: A female w her cubs. They sta with her until they are able to find th own food.

SWEET-TOOTHED BEARS

Bears are **omnivorous**, which means that they eat plants as well as meat. They devour huge quantities of berries, fruit, roots, shoots, and nuts.

They are very sweet-toothed, and they like honey a lot. With their heavy paws, they break open beehives in search of sweet food. They also tear off the bark of trees to catch insects and eat their larvae.

Occasionally they catch rodents, birds, fish, and domestic animals, and they do not turn their noses up at carrion. The largest bears, thanks to their great strength, can kill large mammals (e.g., deer). For this reason, their diets are extremely varied, although plants are their principal source of food.

The polar bear is one exception, because it mostly eats seals and fish, and therefore is a **carnivore**.

Bears use their well-developed sense of smell to locate food. Their sight, in contrast, is not very good.

Some bears are most active in the morning, whereas others prefer to come out at dusk and rest during the day, hidden among vegetation, in trees, or in a cave.

They generally roam alone, covering long distances in their search for food. Even so, in areas where food is abundant, several bears can congregate in the same place.

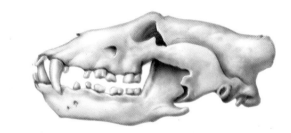

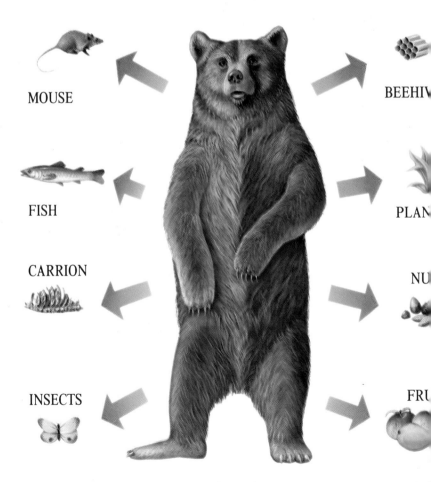

Right: Bears mostly eat roots, shoots, and leaves.

Left: A bear's teeth and jawbone are suitable for eating any type of food. They have long canines for meat and wide molars for chewing vegetation.

MOUSE

FISH

CARRION

INSECTS

BEEHIVE

PLANT

NUT

FRUIT

WINTER SLEEP

In winter, when food is scarce and the temperature drops sharply, some bears spend the coldest months "sleeping" in a refuge. It is not real **hibernation**, because the body temperature, respiration, and metabolic rhythm barely fall. At the slightest danger, they wake up quickly.

During this period, bears do not eat, and live off the fat reserves they have built up during autumn. They usually hide in caves, in hollows between rocks, in hollow tree trunks, or between tree trunk roots. Inside the bear's **den**, the temperature is higher than outside. When good weather comes, they emerge from their den and in a short time regain the weight they had lost. The females emerge with their new cubs that have been born during the winter.

Species that live in warm climates, where food is plentiful all year-round and the temperatures are not extreme, do not undergo the period of winter sleep.

Usually each bear occupies a territory, sometimes big, sometimes small, which it defends from other bears. Bears mark their terrain with olfactory signals: with urine and by rubbing certain **glands** against a surface (e.g., rocks). They also leave marks by tearing the bark off trees with their claws. Sometimes there are confrontations between bears in defense of territory, or over a female.

Left: Bears in colder regions undergo a period of winter **torpor**. During this time they do not eat, but live off the fat reserves they have accumulated during autumn.

Above: These mammals mark th[e] territory by makin[g] scratches on the trunks of trees and by rubbing their glands against roc[ks].

Right: To intimida[te] their rivals, bears growl loudly.

BEARS GREAT AND SMALL

Bears belong to the order *carnivora* and the family *Ursidae*. Many scientists include the giant panda in this family, whereas others place it in the same class with the raccoon and the coati (*Procyonidae*). Some even think that pandas should be placed in a separate family.

Bears live in woods and meadows, in damp forests, and also in high mountains like the Himalayas. The brown bear (the grizzly bear and the Kodiak bear) and the American black bear live in North America. In Europe, there are also brown bears, though few in number. In Asia, there are various species: the Malayan bear, the Asiatic black bear, and the sloth bear.

In South America, only the spectacled or Andean bear is found, and in the cold regions of the Arctic, the polar bear resides.

The size of bears varies a great deal, although most bears are medium size. The biggest bears are the Kodiak and the polar bears. An adult male can reach 10 feet (3 m) long and weigh over 1,323 pounds (600 kg).

Bears have been exterminated from many areas, and in other areas where they were once plentiful, they are now scarce. Unless they are protected, many bear types will one day become extinct. Controlling hunting, protecting young bears, and preserving their **habitats** are some of the measures that must be taken to conserve them.

Right: A Kodiak bear, which is found in the islands of the same name.

Left: An Asiatic black bear (A), a raccoon (B), a giant panda (C), and a red panda (D).

Below: Map of the distribution of bears around the world.

SPECTACLED BEAR

AMERICAN BLACK

MALAYAN BEAR

POLAR BEAR

SLOTH BEAR

ASIATIC BLACK BEAR

BROWN BEAR

A

B

C

D

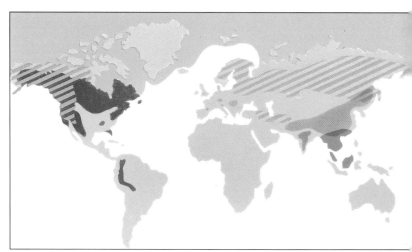

A HUMPBACKED FISHERMAN

The brown bear lives in mountainous forests and also on the great prairies of Europe, Asia, and North America.

The brown bear is a large, thick-furred animal whose color varies from chestnut to silvery, golden gray, and from black to light brown.

Normally the tips of its **fur** tend to be lighter, almost yellowish in color. It has a type of hump between its shoulders, which makes its shape very distinctive.

It is a solitary, territorial animal. At night, it covers large distances, whereas during the day, it prefers to rest in a sheltered place.

Like most bears, the brown bear eats fruit, grass, and roots, although it also eats insects, mammals, fish, and other animals. When the salmon swim upriver every year to their spawning grounds, bears gather there waiting to catch them.

The brown bear is an excellent fisher and catches its prey with a rapid, accurate lash of its claw.

Although this **species** is the most numerous and widespread of the bear family, there was a time when they were even more common. In Europe, very few brown bears are left, except in certain regions of the Russian Republic. North American brown bears include the frightening grizzly bear, which is bigger than its European cousin. But the brown bear is nevertheless bigger than the Kodiak bear, which lives in Alaska.

Right: Brown bears catch the salmon with their teeth or claws and remove the flesh from the bone before eating them.

Below: The first brown bear shakes itself after a swim; the second, a Kodiak, growls; and the third, a grizzly, licks itself. In the middle picture, the unmistakable hump can be seen.

GOING WHERE THEY PLEASE

In the forests in most of the United States and Canada lives another **species** of bear, the American black bear. Despite its name, some have brown or reddish **fur**. Some are even almost white. At present, the American black bear occupies many areas where its American cousin the brown bear used to live.

The American black bear is a very well-known bear in North America, and often lives in national parks where sometimes it is attracted by the food of tourists.

On occasion, the males can cover areas of up to 965 miles (600 km) in search of food or to find the few available females. In some areas, the American black bear has become used to the presence of humans, and even ranges close to human habitation or can be seen on roads, although it is always cautious. It mostly eats plants, but it also catches small animals.

It easily climbs trees to look for fruit. In spring, it can be found roaming on the banks of rivers and it does not hesitate to attack beavers, trying to catch them before they hide in their impregnable lairs. The American black bear, like other bears, spends the winter hidden in a **den**. Sometimes it wakes up and even ventures outside, though only briefly, before returning to the shelter to resume its **hibernation**.

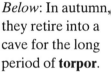

Right: The black American bear is mostly a herbivore but it will eat a beaver if the opportunity presents itself.

Left: Some American black bears have become accustomed to the presence of humans and they can occasionally be seen walking along the street.

Below: In autumn, they retire into a cave for the long period of **torpor**.

A BEAR WITH A MASK

The spectacled or Andean bear is the only **species** of bear that lives in South America. It lives along the length of the Andes mountain range, from Venezuela to Bolivia.

It prefers wet forests, though it can also be found in high prairies, above 9,843 feet (3,000 m).

The spectacled bear has a short snout and its fur is black or dark brown. On its chest and around its eyes it has white patches, like a mask, that give it a very strange appearance. These colorings vary a lot between each bear.

It can climb trees easily and spends a lot of time high up in the branches eating or resting.

Right: The spectacled bear is not completely solitary and at times it forms small groups that feed from the branches of the same tree.

Left: The two rings around the eyes sometimes are joined to the white patch on the chest.

It is basically **vegetarian**, but occasionally it catches insects and other animals.

Unlike other species of bear, **mating** can take place at any time of year. The female usually gives birth to between one and three young per litter. The cubs are very small and defenseless when they are born and they are looked after by the mother.

The spectacled bear is very timid and cautious, and it avoids the presence of humans. Perhaps it is for this reason that very little is known of its habits.

Today, its numbers have diminished a great deal, most of all because of hunting and because its **habitat** has been destroyed by man.

Left: Map of the distribution of the only bear that lives in South America.

LIFE ON THE ICE

The polar bear lives on islands, along the length of the coast and on moving blocks of ice in the Arctic. It has a long snout and neck and a small, narrow head.

It is very well adapted to the difficult and **inhospitable** environment in which it lives. Its dense, impermeable fur, its thick skin, and an abundant layer of fat protect it from the cold, both in and out of the water.

It moves over the ice with no problem because it has **fur** on the soles of its feet that stops it from slipping. It is an excellent swimmer, propelling itself with its forelegs, and it also dives

Right: The mother remains seated wh her young suckle.

Above: After tracking down its favorite food, a sea the bear breaks the ice to reach it.

below the water well. It can stay in icy water for hours.

The polar bear does not keep to fixed territory, but roams over wide areas. It has been seen swimming among blocks of floating ice, several miles from the coast.

It is an excellent hunter. It mainly eats seals, but it also catches fish and seabirds and it salvages the remains of dead whales. Only occasionally does it eat vegetation.

In winter, the female moves away from the coast and prepares a den under the snow. It hollows out a tunnel that ends in a secluded, quiet chamber. Here its young are born, normally two, which already have fur.

Left: The polar bea swims using its forelegs as oars, an it also dives below the water.

A MANE WITH A COLLAR

In its wild state, the Asiatic black bear lives in mountainous forests in many parts of Asia: Pakistan, China, the Himalayan area, and Japan. In summer, it can be found above a height of 9,843 feet (3,000 m), whereas in winter, it comes down to the valleys, where it is easier to find food.

Its body is covered in thick black **fur**, which has a white fringe in the form of a V or a Y decorating its chest.

Around its neck and shoulders, the fur is longer and thicker, making a mane around the throat. This makes it seem more **corpulent** than it really is.

The Asiatic black bear has large, round ears, but its claws are very short.

Although it mainly eats vegetation—fruit, nuts, roots—this **species** also eats meat. In populated areas, it sometimes attacks cattle and can kill animals as big as a horse.

It is a good climber and often climbs trees, both to look for food and to rest between the foliage. In summer, it sleeps or rests on platforms that it makes in the trees with the branches that it breaks when it is eating.

Right: During autumn, when it has to build up fat reserves for winter, it attacks animals such as this dormouse.

Above: In summer, the Asiatic black bear makes platforms in the trees with the branches it breaks when it is eating.

Right: Two bear cubs playing.

Right: Its brilliant, black fur has a very distinctive V- or Y-shaped mark on the chest.

A TERMITE EATER

In the wet forests of India, Nepal, and Sri Lanka lives a very strange bear—the sloth bear. This bear is unique among its **species**.

It has a white snout that is long and hairless. It can move and stick out its lips. With the help of its snout, lips, and tongue, it makes a type of tube that allows it to suck up ants and termites, which form its main source of food.

It can also shut its nostrils if it wants to, so that soil or insects do not go up its nose. Its claws are very long and curved, and can cause deep scratches or can help it hang upside down.

The sloth bear eats insects, sugarcane, fruit, and flowers, and other plants. However, what it likes most are insects. The thick, solid nests that these insects construct does not manage to keep the sloth bear out, because it is well equipped to break them open.

With strong lashes of its claws, it makes a hole in the termites' nest, and then blows to clear the soil from the opening it has made. Next it sucks up the nest's inhabitants—adults, larvae, and eggs. It is said that the noise that this makes can be heard 328 feet (100 m) away.

Above: The female usually has two young in a shelter dug out from the ground. The young leave the lair when they are two or three months old, but they do not leave their mother for a year or two.

Right: A sloth bear eating its favorite food: termites.

Left: This bear is distinguishable by long snout, its hairless lips, and its impressive claws.

THE SMALLEST OF ALL

The Malayan bear is the smallest representative of the bear family. It measures about 4 feet, 7 inches (140 cm) long and weighs about 132 pounds (60 kg).

Its **fur** is velvety black and very short. On its chest, it has a bright mark the shape of a horseshoe. Its snout is short and dexterous.

With its curved claws it tears the bark from trees in search of insects, which it catches with its long, extendible tongue.

The Malayan bear has no hair on the soles of its paws, so it can climb trees easily.

It mostly eats vegetables and it likes honey very much. It also catches insects and small **vertebrates**. Like the sloth bear, the Malayan likes ants and termites.

It lives in thick forests in southeast Asia and in tropical and subtropical equatorial areas, so it never undergoes a period of **torpor**.

It spends most of its time high up in the trees, which it climbs with ease in its search for food. During the day, it likes to rest among the branches, lying in the sun. During the night, it is particularly active...

Above: This small bear likes ants very much, so it happily empties the ants from their nest.

Right: A Malayan bear climbing a tree and another lying in the sun on a platform made from broken branches, several feet above the ground.

Left: To climb trees easily, the soles of feet have no hair.

Far Left: Two adult bears fighting for territory.

OF BEARS AND MEN

Adult bears have few natural predators, but the young are much more vulnerable and are in danger of being attacked by large **carnivores** like wolves or pumas.

The bear's greatest enemy is, as always, humankind. These magnificent creatures have been persecuted since ancient times. They are hunted for their meat and for their valuable **fur**. They are also a precious trophy among hunters.

The destruction of their **habitat** is another of the reasons why the number of bears has fallen so much. Usually they avoid humans and run away when they sense them nearby.

However, bears can be very dangerous on account of their large size and great strength. When they feel threatened, either personally or for their cubs, or when they are wounded or hungry, they can be extremely aggressive and can attack ferociously, causing serious wounds and even death.

In some regions, bears come close to human habitation in search of food and they damage crops, destroy beehives, and attack cattle. Sometimes they can even be found at garbage dumps, scavenging among the garbage.

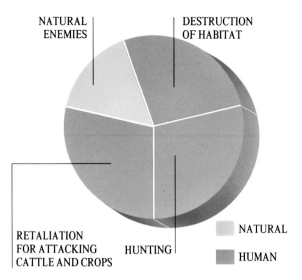

NATURAL ENEMIES

DESTRUCTION OF HABITAT

RETALIATION FOR ATTACKING CATTLE AND CROPS

HUNTING

NATURAL

HUMAN

Right: If a bear cub finds itself alone, it can be attacked by a pack of wolves.

Left: The main reasons for the disappearance of bears are caused by humans.

Left and Below: Hunters follow bears' tracks, interpreting the marks that they leave behind them: feces, broken branches, stripped bark.

Below: Sometimes garbage offers food

GLOSSARY

carnivore: An animal that eats meat, or can eat meat.

corpulent: Large-bodied.

den: A cave where a bear retreats for shelter and to produce its young.

fur: The form and quality of an animal's skin.

gland: An organ of the body that secretes substances that are either useless or toxic.

habitat: Part of the physical surroundings in which an animal lives.

hibernation: The period of inactivity that some animals undergo in order to be able to survive the adverse conditions of winter. During this period, body temperature falls and there is a general decrease in metabolic functions.

inhospitable: An uncomfortable, unwelcoming location.

mating: The male and the female of the same species come together to produce offspring.

omnivore: An animal that eats all types of organic substances.

plantigrade: An animal that walks by pressing the whole of the soles of its feet on the ground.

species: A group of animals or plants that have a series of characteristics in common that make them similar to each other, and that distinguish them from other species.

torpor: The state of lethargy into which some animals fall during certain periods of the year.

vegetarian: An individual or animal that eats only vegetable matter.

vertebrate: An animal that has a skeleton with a spinal column and a skull.

NDEX

le, 4
's nest, 26
s, 24, 26
nerican black bear,
2, 16
iatic black bear, 12

k, 4, 10
ıver, 16
chive, 8, 28
ds, 8, 20
wn bear, 12, 14, 16

ines, 8
nivorous, 8, 12, 28
rion, 8
tle, 22, 28
vs, 4, 10, 24, 26
nate, 10
pulence, 4, 22
ps, 28

ı, 6, 10

digitigrade, 4

fish, 8, 14, 20
fur, 4, 14, 16, 26

giant panda, 12
glands, 10
grizzly bear, 12, 14
growl, 6, 10

habitat, 12, 18, 28
herbivore, 16
hibernation, 6, 10,
   16
honey, 8, 26
horse, 22
humpbacked, 14

insects, 8, 14, 18, 24, 26

jawbone, 8

Kodiak bear, 12, 14

larvae, 8, 24

Malayan bear, 12, 26
mammal, 4, 8, 14
mane, 22
mating, 6, 18
molars, 8

olfactory signals, 10
omnivorous, 8

period of torpor, 10, 26
pheromones, 12
plantigrade, 4
polar bear, 12, 20
Procyonidae, 12
puma, 28

red panda, 12
rivals, 6
rubbish dumps, 28

salmon, 14

seal, 20
sight, 8
sloth bear, 12, 24, 26
smell, 8
spectacled bear, 12, 16
sweet-toothed, 8

termites, 24, 26
territory, 10, 28
torpor, 16, 26
tracks, 28

unguligrade, 4
Ursidae, 12

vegetation, 8, 16, 20,
   24, 26
vegetarian, 18, 22
vertebrate, 26

whale, 20
winter rest, 10
wolf, 28